PARMENIDES AND EMPEDOCLES

PARMENIDES AND EMPEDOCLES

The Fragments in Verse Translation

by STANLEY LOMBARDO

WIPF *&* STOCK · Eugene, Oregon

For Wm Levitan
and Judy Roitman

Wipf and Stock Publishers
199 W 8th Ave, Suite 3
Eugene, OR 97401

Parmenides and Empedocles
The Fragments in Verse Translation
By Parmenides, and Empedocles,
Copyright©1982 by Lombardo, Stanley
ISBN 13: 978-1-61097-162-1
Publication date 12/21/2010
Previously published by Grey Fox Press, 1982

Contents

PREFACE

The common view of the pre-Socratic philosophers is that they stand at the beginning of Greek (and therefore Western) rationalism and science. And so they do. But they also stood at the end of a tradition, a life of the mind and spirit that was intuitive and holistic. Men like Pythagoras, Heraclitus, Parmenides and Empedocles did not distinguish science from poetry or religious experience from philosophical understanding. They represent an older cultural type—in many ways they resemble Siberian and American Indian shamans—that disappeared from the Greek world in the classical period, and is perhaps not widely enough understood in our own time.

E. R. Dodds and others, following the lead of the Swiss scholar Karl Meuli, have traced the outlines of a Greek shamanistic tradition that had contact with Asiatic shamanism in Scythia, was evidenced in the eastern Aegean rim and in Crete, and crossed over to southern Italy in the sixth century B.C. with Pythagoras. Parmenides, from Elea in southern Italy, was in this line; and Empedocles, a Sicilian, was its last representative.

A shaman is trained to undertake hazardous spiritual journeys in order to exercise compassion and advance in wisdom, and he often reports his experiences in the form of a song, chant or poem. Parmenides' poem closely resembles such a report, both in the details of the journey recounted in the prologue and in the substance of what the Goddess tells him, which is that the universe and our minds form a mutually committed whole. Dodds calls Empedocles' fragments "the one first-hand source from which we can still form some notion of what a Greek sha-man was really like" (*The Greeks and the Irrational* [1951], p. 145). His understanding of the physical and the meta-physical universe was directed toward a personal transfor-mation that enabled him to benefit others and realize his own liberation. Poetry was for both of them a natural, but practiced, means of expression. They were not philoso-phers who just happened to write in verse.

Alongside their poetic practice I think both Empedocles and Parmenides trained themselves in some kind of formal meditation practice, perhaps Pythagorean in origin, and that there are hints of what this was in the fragments. I have indicated in the Introductions what can be made of this. The historical record, scant at best for both Parmen-ides and Empedocles, is not helpful here. But their poetry exists; it can be pieced together still, and through the pieced vision we can understand something of their minds.

PARMENIDES

INTRODUCTION

> Parmenides seems to me, in the words of Homer, a
> man toward whom one feels reverence tinged with
> awe. When I was but a youth and he a very old man I
> conversed with him, and he struck me as having a
> wonderful depth of mind. I fear that perhaps we fail
> to understand what he was saying, and still more his
> reasons for saying it. (Socrates, in Plato's *Theaetetus*,
> 183B)

I fear the same thing, and with more reason than Socrates,
but I have a strong missionary spirit toward classical
poetry languishing in the tenement housing of prose
translations. One of the reasons why no one has come
along to rescue the fragments of Parmenides' poem is that
his interpreters have until recently slighted, ignored, or
misunderstood the poetic form in which this early fifth
century mystic-philosopher expressed his dual and con-
trasting vision of the ultimate nature of reality and a theo-
retical physical model of that reality. Philosophers from
Plato to Giorgio de Santillana have sifted out the logical
and metaphysical implications of Parmenides' text, but
Alexander Mourelatos' study (*The Route of Parmenides*,
Yale, 1970) was the first to recognize the importance of
analyzing the fragments as fragments of a poem. Others
had pointed out the Homeric and Hesiodic overtones of
Parmenides' hexameters and acknowledged the likelihood
that he was working in a tradition of Orphic or shamanistic
poetry. But it was Mourelatos' sensitivity to image, metaphor, and verbal and metrical nuance that marked the
resurrection of Parmenides as a poet. The interpretation of

Parmenides' poem implicit in my translation differs from Mourelatos' interpretation (and most others) in important respects. But interpretation of a text such as Parmenides' is primarily a matter of emphasis. My hope is simply that the poem which I, as an added artificer, have made out of Parmenides' Greek will contribute to the reinstatement of his text as poetry.

In making over the twenty fragments of Parmenides' philosophical epic the translator is assisted by the contemporary poetic convention that fragments take on an enhanced significance by their very fragmentary nature. Everyone who works with Parmenides in any way must be tempted to alter the arrangement of the fragments provided by Diels in his standard edition. I certainly tried to do so. In the end I was impressed with the poetic sense of Diels' order and retained it for that reason. This also facilitates comparison with the Greek text and with the standard prose translations. It would be interesting to experiment with versions that run the fragments together, reassemble them or imbed them in the matrix of another poem, but I have not done any of these things here. Parmenides' fragments very happily constitute a poem for us in their traditional scholarly arrangement.

What I have done with the Greek text is to radicalize it at certain points in the spirit of what I see to be the poem's fundamental orientation. I say "radicalize" rather than "take liberties" or some such euphemism because the intent of my transformations is to get to the heart of the text and create an English version out of what I find there. The process begins in the first four lines:

> The horses that take me to the ends of my mind
> were taking me now: the drivers had put me
> on the road to the Goddess, the manifest Way
> that leads the enlightened through every delusion.

The phrases "ends of my mind," "the enlightened," and "through every delusion" will surprise the reader familiar with the Greek text. Let me explain two of these before indicating the underlying interpretation.

"The enlightened" for *eidota phota* (literally, the "knowing man") plays on the word *phos* (a homonym for "man" and "light") in the same way as Parmenides himself does in fr. 14. There the Homeric tag *allotrios phos* is transferred to the wandering moon with her borrowed (foreign, not her own) light.

"Delusion" is a literal translation of the manuscript reading *atē*. The manuscript tradition is corrupt here, for *atē* is grammatically impossible, but no one is really happy with the commonly accepted emendation *astē* ("cities"): there is no manuscript authority for it, and it trivializes Parmenides' experience as that of philosopher on tour. I have therefore simply translated the manuscript reading.

Most readers will have little difficulty accepting the rationale of these translations. "Ends of my mind" is more radical, creating an interior psychological space out of the literal "as far as my desire reaches." I have done this because I want to suggest that Parmenides' poem is concerned with a unique inner experience, the encounter of one's mind with Being and the realization that they are the same. The road that leads to this experience is therefore a

"Way," a spiritual path rather than a logical route or an analytical method.

In vocabulary, meter and style Parmenides' Greek is in the tradition of Homeric and Hesiodic epic verse. But the main thrust of the prologue takes us out of familiar Greek territory, beyond Homeric travel fantasy and Hesiod's mythic cosmogony, into another world where the operant tradition is shamanistic. Shamanistic cultures still exist in many tribal societies, particularly in Siberia where they have been widely studied, and have left traces of their past existence over a very wide area, including the Greek world during the archaic period. It is possible to trace, as E. R. Dodds has done, a tentative line of Hellenic shamanistic descent which has the Thracian Orpheus as its mythological prototype and begins historically in Scythia in the seventh century B.C. when the Black Sea was first opened to Greek trade and colonization—the principal figures here are Abaris and Aristeas—then crosses the Hellespont into Asiatic Greece, emigrates with Pythagoras in the sixth century to southern Italy (where it may have already arrived by another route), and is last represented personally in the fifth century by Empedocles, the extravagant Sicilian philosopher, poet, wonderworker and healer. Parmenides, a native of Elea in southern Italy, was himself a Pythagorean and exerted a strong influence on Empedocles: in the line we are tracing he is associated with shamanistic figures both as teacher and student. The details of the journey narrated in his poem's prologue are paralleled in the reports of Siberian shamans who, among their other powers, have the ability to project their souls, sometimes conveyed by horses and with female guides, through the sky (often through portals of some kind) or into cosmic space, during which journeys they acquire special knowledge from spirits or divine beings.

But the poem's shamanistic element, though germane and generative of much of the prologue's unusual energy, is, like the epic style, ultimately only a mode of expression for Parmenides, who is not interested in any special role for himself. The effect of the shamanistic style is to lead us to regard as a spiritual path the road to Being that the Goddess points out in the subsequent fragments and not to misconstrue her teaching as a method of logical reasoning. This is, I think, the misunderstanding that Socrates hinted at. The poem is experiential, not analytical; the Goddess' teaching is aimed at leading the listener to experience "the still heart of Truth, unconcealed and committed." But there is a sequel: she also teaches him "the world as interpreted by human opinion," which is inherently erroneous, and yet he will learn that this world too is the same as his own mind. And there is a hint of the consequences which this realization entails. The poem fulfills the promise implicit in its opening lines, taking the reader on an interior journey to the ends of his mind, along a road that leads through every delusion. But it is a road that must be learned.

Fragments 2 through the middle of 8 constitute the first part of the Goddess' teaching, known in Parmenidean scholarship as the Way of Truth. She begins (fragment 2) by distinguishing two roads, one leading directly to what Is, the other denying that there Is anything at all. The choice between the two is critical; she returns to it in fragments 6, 7, and 8, sternly warning her pupil not to proceed down the road to Nothingness, which is "not a true route" at all and "will never break through" to the truth. The truth is that What Is does exist, and that it is identical with one's own mind.

The single line that constitutes fragment 3 is the heart of the teaching: "for to think and to be are one and the same." "To think" here translates the Greek verb *noein*, which signifies a direct, intuitive kind of thinking rather than a process of reasoning. It is the function of the mind whereby we perceive a thing's essential nature, and although it can be put out of commission temporarily it cannot, when functioning, be mistaken. It is this faculty— *noein*—direct perception—that the Goddess wants her pupil to direct towards Being. In fragment 4 she gives him a meditation exercise in which he is to fix his *noos* ("mind," the noun form of *noein*) steadily on what is not physically present until he perceives that for *noos* the world is undifferentiated: Being stands alone in its unity yet is somehow diffused through the universe.

We are being prepared for an ultimate encounter with pure Being, but first there are warnings of two other false roads besides the road to nothingness. In fragment 6 we are barred from "the road the witless wander," the meandering, retrograde road that most people travel through life, without any strong commitment to reality. The other road barred is the empirical road (fragment 7), which proceeds inductively from sense data and so is inherently defective. Neither of these is the road to Being. That road is finally described in the long fragment 8, beginning with a list of the signs marking the route—Uncreated, Undestroyed, Whole, Single, Motionless, Complete—each of which is then examined in succession until finally an image forms and the IT we have been traveling towards appears. The journey in fragment 8 is, until it nears the end, a metaphysical tour, but the space-travel motif of the prologue resumes after the shipboard dialectics and we are again operating on the level of *noos*, direct perception (development of which was the prerequisite for the voyage), and when Being appears it is

> like a Sphere in space
> perfectly round and balanced
> from every perspective
> in precise equipoise.

We have reached the ends of the universe, the limits of our minds, where mind and all Being are One. But though this is apparently the road's end, the journey is not over. We have been traveling at great intensity, as if at lightspeed, with a one-pointedness that precluded awareness of anything but the Reality at the road's end. Now it is necessary to return.

The second part of the Goddess' instruction (end of fragment 8 to the end of the poem) has traditionally been called the Way of Seeming. Her teaching here is "deceptive," based on a dualistic interpretation of the world that has no absolute validity but is necessary nonetheless: it is the way men have "made up their minds" to see the world. The final portion of the poem is very fragmentary. We are left with a pieced vision of a beautiful, complex cosmos with light and darkness, change, the harmony of opposites and, if the harmony is disturbed, the possibility of suffering. The fragments fall naturally into an order that suggests a journey back from the ultimate One that is beyond space and time, and a return into the circles of the world, the milky way and stars, the sun, past the moon, and finally to earth. In the center of this cosmos is

> the daimon who regulates all,
> controls the mingling of bodies, the misery of birth...

and when we return to earth we see a man and a woman making love and witness the formation of an embryo. We sense from these passages the suffering inherent in all birth and becoming and multiplicity, in bodies that have extension and are composite. But there is also a sense of quiet acceptance here and throughout the poem's coda. The suffering of the embryo and the misery of childbirth recall the bonds and constraints upon Being itself:

> strong compulsion upon it
> Ananke binding it...

Being too, is limited, as much an object of compassion as the suffering embryo. It is a strange and awesome conception.

And yet not strange. We begin to realize in an astonishing four-line fragment (16) near the end that our minds are not different from our bodies, and that the ordinary world too, like Being itself, is identical with our minds:

> As crasis of the body, mixture of much-beaten limbs,
> so too is mind for man. It is the body grows to mind.
> All men desire the same thing, apprehend the same
> The plenum is thought, and thought preponderates.

We all desire and apprehend the same thing, and this commonality extends to all there is.

In an isolated fragment (5) near the beginning of the poem the Goddess says:

Where I begin is all one to me
Wherever I begin I will return again

Parmenides' route is not one-way and out. The encounter with the One is not the end: however absolute and irreducible an experience it may seem, it is not validated until it is brought back into the world of everyday life. Wisdom is validated by compassion. We think of Plato's philosopher returning to the cave after seeing the world of light, and of the Taoist-Zen sage who rides the ox back home and mingles with the people of the world.

i

The horses that take me to the ends of my mind
were taking me now: the drivers had put me
on the road to the Goddess, the manifest Way
that leads the enlightened through every delusion.

I was on that road. Wizard mares
strained at the chariot and maidens drove it.
The axle whined in the hubs
                  like a Panspipe
hanging fire in the whirl of the wheels,
                  propulsion
      of these priestess-daughters of the Sun
when they leave on a mission from nightspace to light
pushing their veils from their heads with their hands.

The gates of the skyways of Night and Day
loomed up before us,
                gates made of space-stuff
but capped with a lintel
                a stone threshold before them
and filled with the mass of great solid doors.

Avenging Dikē was there with her retributive keys.

The drivers knew what to say
        their passwords persuaded her
to slide back the bolts
            and the gates flew open
swiveling on pins set in heavy bronze hinges
and creating the vastness of space as they turned.

The maidens drove
        the chariot through
the horses
        stayed on the track

and there was the Goddess
        friendly
        my right hand in hers
        a goddess receiving me

        she saying:

The horses that take you to the ends of your mind
have taken you here, these
        and immortal maidens for charioteers.
Welcome, young man, and be glad:
It is no evil fortune has set you to travel
this road, far from the usual paths of mankind,
        but great Themis and Dikē.
        You are here to be taught,
both the still heart of Truth, unconcealed and committed,
and human Opinion, on which there can be no reliance.
        But you shall also learn this:
how the Interpreted World really does exist,
        all of it one throughout space and time.

ii

I am your teacher. Remember my words.

There are two ways for the seeker to understand the world.

The first is
        IT IS
and that IT ISN'T cannot be.
This route is committed to reality and truth.
The second is
        IT ISN'T
and that IT ISN'T must be.

No information comes back from this road.
You cannot know nonexistence
                which cannot be accomplished
Cannot even speak of it

iii

. . . for to think and to be are one and the same.

iv

            Fix your mind's eye steadily
            on things that are absent
            as though they were present.
            You will find
            you cannot distinguish
            being from being
            nor determine whether
            it is diffused through the cosmos
            or stands singly alone.

v

Where I begin is all one to me
Wherever I begin I will return again

vi

Speaking and thinking are the same as WHAT IS.
              WHAT IS exists
              Nothing does not
              Keep this before you.

I bar you first from this road:
              Do not think of Nothingness.
And I bar you from the road the witless wander,
the splaybrained masses without self-direction,
deaf blind and astounded, the paranoid millions
who compulsively confuse what is with what isn't,
all of them moving on a retrograde road.

vii

That Nothingness exists will never break through.
Withhold your mind from that way of inquiry.
But don't let fashion force you to travel
              the empirical road either
using the blind eye for instrument
                  the ringing ear and the tongue,
but use your mind to respond to my challenge
              and the disturbance it causes.

viii

> . . . and now there remains
only my account of the road to WHAT IS.
Signs there are many:
> > Uncreated
> > Undestroyed
> > Whole
> > Single
> > Motionless
> > Complete

IT never was nor will be, since it IS timelessly now
a continuous One.
> What genesis could you find for what IS?
From what origin grown to what final point?
> *I will not allow you*
to say or to think creation from nothing: IT ISN'T
cannot be spoken or thought. If IT started from nothing
what stirred it to being, and why sooner than later?
IT must BE totally or not be at all.
The force of commitment will not allow
generation from nothing, and Dikē therefore
does not loosen her bonds
to permit birth or destruction
but holds fast. Here again is the critical
IT IS or IT ISN'T, and our decision has been
to leave the latter unnamed, an unknowable nothing,
not a true route at all,
and to affirm the former as the authentic Way.
Being does not *get* to be, either in time past or future:
It would not BE if it did.

In this way
        birth is snuffed out and destruction unheard of.

IT is indivisible, an homogeneous whole,
not more in one place
                which would prevent its coherence
and less in another

                a plenum of existence
continuous gravitation of being towards being.

IT is motionless too: locked into its boundaries
IT neither starts nor stops,
birth and destruction
beaten away by our commitment to Truth,
but self-contained and perfectly one with itself
IT remains firmly There, strong compulsion upon it
Anankē binding it
to rest in its boundaries.
Nor will Themis allow that IT be incomplete.
IT would be totally deficient if deficient at all.
IT is There to be known, the *why* of all thinking.
You will not find thought unsupported by Being
                thought is committed to Being
and nothing is nor will be apart from WHAT IS
since Moira has bound it to be whole and still.
It is for IT that names are devised,
all the categories men use, thinking them true
birth and destruction
                being and non-being
locomotion and change
                all the bright shifts of surface.

But since IT is bounded it must be complete

> like a sphere in space
> perfectly round and balanced
> from every perspective
> in precise equipoise

not more of it here or less of it there
since the void of nothingness does not exist
to fracture its wholeness, nor can Being exceed
or fall short of itself,
> an inviolate whole
equal to itself in every direction,
uniformly present within its bounds.

Here ends my discourse and thoughts about Truth.
Trust what I have said. But now you must learn
of the World as interpreted by human Opinion.
Listen to the deceptive order of my words.

Men have made up their minds to name two kinds of forms
(an erroneous decision: one shouldn't be named)
which they distinguish as opposites, zoning off reality
under separate headings

> here the fire of the sky
> a delicate flame
> running along itself

> and completely distinct

> from its opposite, Night
> brutely dark
> a dense heavy continuum

and so the whole system, consistent throughout,
which I transmit to you here
so that your understanding will be second to none.

ix

When everything has been labeled Darkness and Light
according to their various characteristics,
inilluminable Night fills up the universe
on an equal basis with Light, one as real as the other.

x

You will come to know
the nature of the sky and all the signs that are there,
the imperceptible effects of the sun's blinding rays
and the source of its energy,
the force and the nature of the round-faced moon
in her erratic orbit,
and the arching dome of the universe,
how it originated
and how Necessity engineered it to fetter the stars.

xi

 . . . how earth, sun and moon
the bright common sky and the milky way
and the outer edge of olympos rose into being
and the fierce heat of the stars

xii

The tight inner orbits
are filled with pure fire,
then the flame dies down
and the circles grow dark.
In the center the daimon who regulates all,
controls the mingling of bodies, the misery of birth.
She sends the female to mate with the male,
the male with the delicate female.

xiii

Eros first of all the gods she devised

xiv

nightshining
          round earth
a wanderer with borrowed light

xv

          forever
glaring at the rays of the sun

xv^a

rooted in water

xvi

As crasis of the body, mixture of much-beaten limbs,
so too is the mind for man. It is the body grows to mind
all men desire the same thing, apprehend the same
The plenum is thought, and thought preponderates.

$xvii$

male [embryos] on the right, female on the left

$xviii$

Man and woman mixing the seeds of love,
mingling bloods: if this energy is harmonious
the new body forms well
but if conflicts arise and the sexual force is divided
the embryo suffers

xix

This is the world in common Opinion,
things coming to be and passing away in their season,
and to everything men have given
a distinctive name.

EMPEDOCLES

INTRODUCTION

> Homer and Empedocles have nothing in common
> except for their meter. If the one is to be called a poet,
> the other should be called a natural philosopher
> rather than a poet. (Aristotle, *Poetics* 1447)

Aristotle is quibbling, dissembling, or both. In a less cele-
brated passage (*On Poets*, fr. 70) he gives credit to Empedocles' sense of metaphor, powerful phrasing, and poetic
technique in general. In any case, philosophical poetry
was, then as now, a major form; and Empedocles' texts
would be recognized as poetry—by the sheer energy of
his language if nothing else—whether they were in meter
or not. That they have not been so recognized by our liter-
ary generation is simply a matter of where and how trans-
lators have been directing their energies.

Recognition in antiquity was immediate and lasting,
both for the man and his poetry. Empedocles (c. 490–c. 430
B.C.) was a Western Greek from the old and culturally rich
soil of Sicily. Politically active (to the point of exile) in his
native city Akragas, he was in touch with the philosophical
and religious movements percolating through the larger
Greek world and in particular those that emanated from
southern Italy, home to Pythagoras and Parmenides and a
center of mystic religious activity. He lived during the
Golden Age of Pericles, but spiritually he belonged to an
earlier generation; and although he never visited Athens,
his reputation as a philosopher-shaman was pan-Hellenic.

It was a reputation founded at least partly on his poetry.
His *Purifications*, a poem which would be a classic of personal religious literature if we had more if it, awed the

crowds at Olympia when it was recited at the festival there by a professional rhapsode. The performance was enhanced by a personal appearance by the master himself, conspicuous even at the Olympics in bronze sandals, purple cloak and flowering wreath, his customary public apparel. But his appeal was more than popular, and it extended beyond his own lifetime. The Alexandrian critic Dionysius Thrax, who wrote what were to become standard handbooks of rhetoric, ranked Empedocles with Pindar and Aeschylus for the "austere and difficult harmony" of his poetic style. And the passionate but nononsense Roman poet Lucretius eulogized Empedocles as a culture hero and imitated his style in his own philosophical epic. Nietzsche, Matthew Arnold and T. S. Eliot are among his more recent admirers. Whatever truth there is in the stories about his death—that he leaped into Aetna to prove his immortality or was assumed into heaven by a glittering light above it—he is due a modest rebirth in our time.

We possess some 450 lines of Empedocles' poetry— more text than for any other pre-Socratic philosopher. This material has come down to us in the mode of transmission usual for the pre-Socratics—chance quotation in later authors—as 153 fragments of two long hexameter poems, originally about 3000 lines long each, with the titles *On Nature* and *Purifications*. Assignation of the fragments to one poem or the other is frequently more a matter of judgment than record. As with Parmenides' fragments I have followed Diels' edition, because it is sensible and standard and because there is little to be gained by rearrangement. Empedocles' 150-odd fragments cannot be made to cohere

with the rare formal elegance we find in Parmenides' nine-
teen pieces. But even among the most scattered ruins the
mind of the artificer often still lingers.

Empedocles was in his prime (c. 450 B.C.) about
twenty-five years after Parmenides, whose work he knew
first-hand, and about fifty years after Heraclitus, whose
writings he could not have seen but with whose ideas he
seems somehow to have been familiar. Parmenides and
Heraclitus had defined the polar limits of metaphysics,
Parmenides insisting on the primacy of Being and dis-
missing all becoming and change as illusion, Heraclitus
disavowing any kind of permanence except for that of per-
petual flux. Empedocles had it both ways. His perception
was that becoming without Being is meaningless, and that
Being without becoming is a cosmic bore. To accommodate
both he devised a cyclical physics: four immutable elements (Earth, Air, Water, Fire) operated upon by two op-
posing forces (Love and Strife) combine and disperse to
produce, in alternating phases, the harmonious One and
the divergent Many. Empedocles owed his vision of the
One to Parmenides, and it is a strong, central vision:

> . . . in the densely-patterned
> abyss of space, there
> at the point of fixity
> in the stillness only
> a Sphere, a globe
> quietly rejoicing in its solitude.

But he himself was much more the poet of the Many in all
its manifestations and transmogrifications. *On Nature* pro-
liferated with the details of the physical universe, from the

primordial explosion of the One down to the evolution of the minutest processes of biological organisms. We have enough remnants of this material to be able to appreciate Empedocles' pioneering efforts as a cosmologist, physicist, naturalist, and physiologist. But there is more to appreciate here than embryonic science. Empedocles was a practitioner, not merely a theoretician; and *On Nature* is not just a didactic poem, but an act of transmission.

The transmission was to Pausanias, the poem's addressee and Empedocles' only student (although he had followers and admirers to spare). Pausanias is later heard of as a physician who treated victims of the great plague in Athens (429–428 B.C.), and medicine was part of the practice transmitted by Empedocles, but not the whole of it. The poem's closing fragments (110, 111) suggest larger powers, including control over the weather and over death itself—but we are still dealing with the repertory rather than the art itself, into which the trainee is initiated near the beginning of the poem:

> And now: Start using every faculty
> to see how each thing is clear. (fr. 4)

This is not merely a recommendation for scientific observation with an eye to formulating theories. Empedocles is not overly concerned with the accuracy of his theories (see fragments 21 and 71). What he wants first, and what his poetic practice consistently demonstrates, is clear perception of the entities that present themselves to our senses and our minds. The knowledge we so receive is admittedly meager in comparison with the Whole (fragment 2), as is the knowledge obtained from formal teaching of any kind, including Empedocles' own (end of fragment 2). This does not matter. It is the sequel, what one does with what one has received, that is important. First,

> shelter it in a silent heart... (fr. 3)

then,

> ... sift these words through the guts of your being.
>
> (fr. 5)

And, finally, when the instruction is complete:

> Press these things into
>   the pit of your stomach
> as you meditate with pure
>   and compassionate mind
> and they will be with you the rest of your life
> and from them much more, for they grow of
> themselves into the essence,
>   into the core of each person's being... (fr. 110)

It is the internalization, or digestion, of the poem's myriad data—of the Many, in fact—that the trainee must accomplish in order to acquire the shamanic powers promised by the master. It is a meditative process that requires purity and compassion, and it is the basis not only for the acquisition but the retention and deepening of the powers. Here is the heart of Empedocles' teaching and practice in *On Nature*. We see the process reflected in the poem's metaphysics—the Many return to the One when Love, centered in the Whorl, becomes the operant force in the universe—and embodied in the poem itself, which even in its fragmented form is largely a sustained meditation on the Becoming of all things.

On Nature is Empedocles' legacy of his knowledge and

art. *Purifications* is his last testament. At some point in his life Empedocles immersed himself in Pythagoreanism, responding not to its mathematical mysticism but to its doctrine of reincarnation and the ethics attendant upon that doctrine. Although Pythagoreanism may not be enough to account for all that is in it, *Purifications* is a thoroughly Pythagorean poem. It is Empedocles' testification—in the tradition of Pythagoras himself, who professed to have recollected a number of his past lives—that he has fully perceived the nature, not of the universe now, but of his own soul, with its history of suffering in previous lives and in its present state of liberation.

We have far fewer pieces of *Purifications* than of *On Nature*, and their order is more problematic. The title refers to purificatory rites of initiation into mysteries. Fragment 143 is probably a reference to ritual purification with water, but it is better to take the title as indicating that the poem as a whole is an act of purification and an initiation into mysteries. Empedocles was accused of being one of the first (with Philolaus) to reveal the secret teachings and practices of the Pythagoreans. It is not unlikely that we have here bits of the first large-scale publicization of such esoteric (to fifth-century Greeks) dogmas as the existence of an occult self, its immortality and metempsychosis, the sinfulness of killing/consuming ensouled beings, and karmic retribution through an individual's successive lives. What is not revealed in our fragments, except perhaps obliquely, is the *askesis*—the spiritual training—that the Pythagoreans undertook. I am not referring to their way of life in general, which we know included communal living, vegetarianism, sexual restrictions, a rule of silence and the use of music as catharsis—but to what is known as Pythagorean "memory-training" (*anamnesis*). The master in fragment 129 is almost certainly Pythagoras, whose "visceral mind" (translation of *prapides*—the mind as located in the upper abdomen) took in each and every existent for ten or even twenty human generations. This is a more developed form—extending through time—of the practice inculcated in *On Nature*, and it may have been part of a Pythagorean practice that led ultimately to self-knowledge in a radical sense, a knowledge that begins with the recollection of the forms the self has already assumed. The transformations that are without any self-nature in *On Nature* have become personal history in *Purifications*:

> I have already been
>   a boy and a girl
>   a bush and a bird
>   a mute fish in the sea. (fr. 117)

The final transformation that Empedocles claims for himself, from mortal man to god, he refuses to regard as "some great accomplishment" (fr. 113). This refusal seems to be not humility—a nonvirtue for Empedocles as for most Greeks—but a recognition that there is in the end, to use Buddhist terms, "no attainment and nothing to attain." The gods exist in bliss as humans exist in suffering; but beyond such differences in state, yet pervading them, there is

> one awesome Mind
>   inexpressibly alone

> riddling the universe
> with its lightspeed thoughts
> . . .
>
> a continuum through the aether
> through the infinite brightness. (frs. 134-135)

Empedocles never forgot Parmenides' One, and when he returns to it here we feel he has liberated it from the bonds and limitations that Parmenides' Goddess insisted were upon it, leaving us with a glimpse of a Mind with no need of purification and a universe without any hindrance in it.

On Nature

1

Listen, Pausanias,
             son of Ankhitos the Sage:

2

Our bodies are tunneled
             with myopic sense organs,
stimuli bombard us, pain
             blunts the mind's edge.
We glimpse our momentary share of existence

and with lightning doom
             drift up like smoke and disperse

each one believing
             only what he's met in his random encounters
and proudly imagining to have found

             the Whole.

Well, it can't be seen
             not in this way
             can't be heard
cannot be grasped by the human mind.

And you, on this retreat, will learn
no more than human thought can attain

3

but shelter it in a silent heart.

4

They're mad, O gods,
                    keep their madness from my tongue!
Siphon a pure spring
                    through my sanctified lips,
                              And you
white-armed virgin whom many would marry
                              Muse of all
that is lawful for mortals to hear:
Drive me in your chariot with its delicate reins
as far as is lawful from Piety's side.
Fame's deathly blossoms
                    could never tempt
                         you, Goddess,
                    to pluck those flowers
          say out of boldness more than what's right
or enthrone yourself upon Wisdom's peaks.

And now: Start using every faculty
                    to see how each thing is clear.
          You have sight, but don't trust it
                    more than your ears,
          nor booming sound
                    more than the probe of your tongue,
          Don't check any of your body's means of perception
          But take constant notice of the clarity of things.

5

And although inferiors mistrust their masters profoundly
you must attain the knowledge
                    our Muse attests to and orders

But first
        sift these words through the guts of your being.

6

Learn first the four roots of all that is:
ZEUS (a white flickering)
                life-breathing HERA
AIDONEUS (unseen)
                and NESTIS
        whose tears form mortality's pool

7

uncreated

8

And I will tell you this:
There is no self-nature
        in anything mortal
        nor any finality
                in death's deconstruction
There is only
                the merging, change
                        and exchange
        of things that have merged
and their self-nature is only
                a matter of words

9

The elements combine and merge,
                form human beast bush or bird

emerging into brilliant air
        but 'originate' is only a word.
And when the elements unsift themselves
        we speak of 'death' & 'sad fate',
language not in accordance with Nature, merely
        a convention, but useful as such, and so

10

    : Death   the avenger

11

But only fools incapable of connected thought
believe that Unbeing can come into being
or that anything that Is
        can pass into nothingness

12

impossible transition
        from Isn't to Is
and for It to be obliterated is wholly absurd:
It will always be There
        where it is fixed forever.

13

No part of the Whole is empty or full

14

and if no emptiness, no room for addition.

15

Nor does the enlightened man
have fantasies at dusk
that only during life
               or what men call life
do we exist
but that after our mortal dissolution
        and before our mortal coalescence
we are as nothing.

16

As these two have been
so will they always be,
nor will infinite Time
ever be empty
of this pair of forces.

17

I will speak in doubles:

At times the solitary One
grows out of Many,
at times the Many out of One.

Genesis is double, and death
double for every mortal thing.
The road to unity
produces and destroys, separation
engenders and the engendered flies apart
in a closed interchange that never ceases:

Union through Love, separation in Strife,
the One overcoming ignorance to be born
out of Many, the Many separating out
from the interval of the One,
neither sure of time when they come into being
but in that their interchange is a ceaseless round,
sure and unmoving in the style of a circle.

Listen to these words
(your mind will grow to their meaning)
and I, as I promised
when revealing to you the ends of my words,
will speak in doubles:

At times the solitary One
grows out of Many, at times
the Many out of One:
                Water, Fire, Earth
                and the steeps of Air.
Apart from them: Hate
                uniformly dense and destructive
and among them: Love
                stretching in every dimension
(look with your mind, don't sit dazed by vision)
                the same Love conceived as innate
                in our mortal bodies, the source
                of harmony in thought and craft,
                called Delight, as Aphrodite praised.
                And although humankind cannot perceive
                her helical dance through the elements

        yet you must observe
        my words' true pattern:

The elements, equal in time and space
but of different valence and character,
predominate in turn
                    in the turning of time.
Nothing besides
                    comes into being or ends,
and their destruction
                    would be the end of all being.
What would there be then
                    to fill up the Whole
and where would it come from?
Where would they go if destroyed
since nothing is empty of them?
No, they are all that there is,
in their interpenetration becoming
different things at different times,
but always themselves, a continuum forever.

                    18

Love

                    19

        tenacious Love

                    20

The human body
            with its structure of limbs
is emblematic of just this process,
all its proper parts
                    brought together through Love

to form one sweet corpus
                    in the flower of youth
then torn apart by discordant forces,
beaten to pieces in the hard surf of life.
So too with trees and shrubs
                    fish in the black water
wild things on the mountainside
          and gulls that skim the water on wings.

21

As substantiation of these colloquys
(assuming a lack of matter
                    in proportion to form)
Observe
the sun, warm
          and luminous in every direction
and the immortal bodies drenched
          in its violet radiance
the raingloom
                    cold over everything
and all the enchanted
          and solid beings
                    that stream from Earth
split by Wrath all of them
          into divergent forms
and coming together in mutual desire and Love.

Here is the origin of what was, is, and will be,
the budding of trees, of men and women both,
beasts and birds and waterspawned fish
and the gods who live for eons in glory.

But the entities alone exist, and though
        in their interpenetration they assume
various modes,
             only so much does mixing change them.

22

The pale gold sun
        Earth, sea and sky
are all in harmony
        with their severed parts
parts that form the bodies of mortal beings.
Things that have a propensity to blend
fall in love for this reason
and are assimilated each to the other
        through Aphrodite's power.
But things that differ from each other most
in origin, composition and modeled form
are not disposed to combine, this hostility due
to the dictates of Hate, who caused their becoming.

23

It is just as when artists paint votive plaques,
master technicians who know their craft well:
They squeeze their polychrome paints in their hands
and mix them proportionately,
        a dab more here, a little less there,
and from the mixture create credible images
of anything you please, peopling a world
with women and men, trees and animals
birds and fish at home in the water

and even the gods who live for eons in glory.

Don't let it escape you: mortal beings
in their manifest and infinite variety
have no different a source.
                              Know this for a fact.
You have a god's word for it.

24

Crest upon crest, and there is no one road
to these words' completion

25

                              Better to say twice
what needs to be said

26

                    The circle revolves
and the elements have their turn into power
fade into each other and grow in their phases.

These are the entities.
                              In their interpenetration
they become humankind and animal domain,
now through Love the symbiosis of one world,
then the diaspora through Hate and Strife,
like a garden grown whole and then turned under.
In that the One has learned to grow from the Many
and the Many to sprout from the decay of the One,
so far are they ephemeral and unsure of time.
But in that their interchange is a ceaseless round,
eternal and unmoving in the style of a circle.

27

Indiscernible from here
the sun's etched limbs
earth's rough mass and seas

but in the densely patterned
abyss of space, there
at the point of fixity
in the stillness only
a Sphere, a globe
quietly rejoicing in its solitude.

27a

not as a society,
with factions and angry moods

28

nor anthropomorphic, with arms
branching out from a back,
feet, supple knees and genitals

29

a perfect sphere
in precise equipoise
eternal
and exulting in its circling solitude

30

But when Hate grown large within its parts
rose to honor at the era's end
ordained for them to alternate

31

            then one by one
the limbs of the god began to quake.

32

One joint binds two

33

            as fig juice
curdles white milk and congeals it

34

Having kneaded a dough of water and barley

35

Returning now to my poem's channel
and coaxing the trickle of my argument:

Hate came to the pit
            of the vortex,

                        Love
to the center of the whorl
and in Love all things came to be One,
slow, yearning beings from every direction,
and from their fusion erupted the 10,000 species.
Yet many things remained unmixed in that crasis,
all that looming Hate checked. Hate had not
wholly withdrawn to the outermost circle:
part still remained, part
                        had left the Sphere's limbs.
But in proportion to its ponderous exodus

a stream of perfect Love, immortal,
compassionate, flowed into the Sphere,
and all was transformed: what had learned
immortality now became mortal,
the pure became mixed,
                    changing their paths,
and from their fusion erupted the 10,000 species
with their manifold forms, marvelous to see.

36

And as they converged Hate took its stand
                    on the outermost edge.

37

First I will list for you
the primeval, coeval elements
origin of all that manifests to our sight:
Earth,
        the swelling sea,
                    moist air,
and titanic aether that envelops the globe.

38

Earth augments her bulk
        aether builds aether

39

If Earth's deeps were endless
        and aether infinitely profuse
as stated in the idle logorrhea of many
who have seen too little of the Whole

40

Helios, the piercing sun,
Selene, the gentle moon

41

Collected, the light moves round the great sky

42

          and obscures its rays
as it passes beneath, covering the Earth
with shade as wide as the grey-eyed moon

43

Sunbeam beating
        the moon's wide disk

44

reflects
      back to Olympos
with glaring face

45

       an alien light
in orbit round Earth

46

     turns
   as a chariot's hub turns, rounding
the goal,

47

    and stares at her lord's
        opposed sacred disk, and

48

Earth makes night

        when it descends with its rays

49

Blind desolate night

50

Rainbow brought wind or storm from the sea

51

Fires flared up

52

        Many smoldered under the ground

53

Chance direction of aether, often changing

54

Aether
    sank its long roots into Earth

55

Earth's sweat, the sea

56

salt
solidified under pressure of sunlight

57

Bulbous heads
                    sprouted in air
                          bare arms
drifted by bereft of shoulders
                                eyes roamed
through space begging for faces

58

limbs wandered alone

59

          as the two gods mingled with each other more
fell together in random collisions
Continuous production of life-forms began

60

pinwheel-footed,
                  a blur of hands

61

       double sternums and brows
    human grafted on bovine
            bovine on human
   and where shadowed limbs meet
androgynous forms emerge and multiply

62

And here an account
          not very far off or uninformed
of how a severed portion of the Fire
       brought to the surface
the midnight tubers of the human race
mere shapeless lumps of earth at first
          compounded of water and warmth
forced up by fire yearning for its like,
still unmanifest the lovely, limbed body,
the voice, and the organ common to men.

63

The dichotomy of birth: part in the man's

64

Desire comes, reminding through sight

65

Poured into the pure, ending in females
when cold is encountered, males when warm

66

into split meadows of Aphrodite

67

Warmer wombs are productive of males
and for this men are darker, hairier
more powerfully built

68

On the tenth day of the eighth month
                            it becomes white pus

69

Bearing twice

70

sheepskin

71

If you are concerned for some substantial proof
of how water, earth, aether, and sun
become in mixture the colors and forms
of all the creatures Aphrodite has knit

72

how tall trees and deepsea fish

73

when the Cyprian goddess
      busy with the forms of things
           sprinkled earth with rainwater
and threw it in the fast fire to harden

74

leading tuneless schools of spawning fish

75

dense inner bodies with spongy outsides
their plasticity molded in Aphrodite's palms

76

shells
the heavy backs of sea-creatures,
conches, stone-hided turtles:
you can see earth living on top of the flesh

77

Perennials clustered with fruit and leaves

78

Proportionate to the air

79

tall olive trees
bearing eggs first

80

                pomegranates
ripen late for this reason
        and apples, juicy so long

81

Water fermented in the wood
                becomes wine from the bark

82

Hair, leaves, thick birdfeathers, scales
on sturdy limbs: all the same

83

but porcupines bristle
with sharp quills on their backs

84

A man about to go out on a stormy night
prepares a lantern, a bright fire enclosed
in linen panels to keep out the wind:
the panels disperse every gust of air
but transmit the fire because it's so much finer
and the beams of light dance and shine on the threshold.
In just this way the primordial fire,
enclosed in gauzy tissue, was lodged in the pupil,
and perforations in the tissue, divinely minute,
blocked the well of water that surrounded the pupil
but transmitted the fire because it was so much finer.

85

The eye's gentle flame received very little earth

86

From which Aphrodite constructed tireless eyes

87

Fitting them with clasps of mutual love

88

One vision generated by two eyes

89

Knowing there are emanations from all that exists

90

So sweet seized sweet, bitter rushed at bitter,
sour went for sour, burning rode upon burning

91

water
compatible with wine, but not with oil

92

copper mixed with tin

93

grey elderberry with flax

94

The blackness of river bottoms arises from shade
and the same thing is seen in cavernous hollows

95

When eyes first took shape in Aphrodite's palms

96

Gentle Earth received in her broad casting-moulds
two parts in eight of dazzling Nestis
and four of Hephaistos. These became white bones
welded together by eerie Harmonia

97

Back-bone

98

Earth lay moored in the perfect harbors of Love
and encountered equal or nearly equal parts
of Hephaistos, cloudwater and glowing aether
and from this came blood and the forms of flesh

99

A bell
          a bough of flesh

Everything breathes in, breathes out:

Bloodless tubes of flesh are strung
along the body's inner wall
and terminate in porous mouths
at the surface of the skin,
a mesh of holes that's drilled so fine
it blocks the blood but lets air in.
So when the silksmooth blood withdraws
the whistling air comes storming through
and when it pulses back again
the air blows out.
                    Think of a child
playing with a shiny bronze clepsydra:
She stops up the tube with her pretty hand
                and dips it in a pool
                of silvery water
                but the liquid blocked
                by the air inside
                pressing down on the sieve
                can't seep into the siphon's bowl
                until she uncovers the thick airstream
                and the escaping air
                is replaced by a proportionate
                volume of water, which
                when it's filled
                the instrument's base
                and the tube's again stoppered
                by human flesh, is checked
                from leaking by the air outside
                straining to get in at the gurgling neck

and controlling the tip
until she lifts her hand:
then the water flows out
as the air falls in.
So with our smooth pounding blood:
when it shoots away into the body's wells
the air streams through in a running swell
and when the blood throbs back, the air exhales.

101

Tracking down with their nostrils the slivers left
by animals' feet on the tender grass

102

So all creatures have a share of scent and breath

103

And all beings think through Luck's sweet will

104

Insofar as the frailest collide as they fall

105

Nourished in the seas of resurging blood:
here is the center of what men call thought
and blood around the heart
is thought for men.

106

The human mind grows toward the present state.

107

All formed things are compacted of these
and through these men think, feel pleasure and grieve.

108

As they change by day
so does their nocturnal thinking change

109

It is through earth we perceive earth,
water through water, through aether
bright aether, consuming fire through fire,
love through love, and hate through grim hate.

110

Press these things into
                    the pit of your stomach
as you meditate with pure
                    and compassionate mind
and they will be with you the rest of your life,
and from them much more, for they grow of themselves
into the essence,
                    into the core of each person's being.
But if your appetite is for all those other things

that generate suffering
                         and blunt human minds
these powers will leave you in the turning of time
and out of love for their own
                         return to the Source.
For this you must know:

All things have intelligence, and a share of thought.

111

You will learn every drug potent
                    against disease and old age
(for you alone I will do this)
and you will stop the force of restless winds
that shred the farmlands when they blow over earth,
and, whenever you wish, bring the breeze back.
           After black rain you will make a seasonable dryness
for human well-being, and after a parching summer,
tree-feeding streams that flow down from the sky.

And you will bring back from Hades a dead man's strength.

Purifications

112

Friends in the great city above the brown Akragas
with homes on the rocky heights, good folk, respectful
harbor of strangers, innocent of evil:
                    I bring you this
formal greeting as an undying god, mortal no longer,
honored by all and fittingly crowned with sacral
ribbons and flowering wreaths. To whatever flourishing
cities I come with my followers here, men and women both,
I am revered, sought by thousands, some inquiring
of the road to wealth, some in need of prophecy,
others trying to hear a healing word for the long
afflictions that pierce their bodies through with pain.

113

But why go on about this, as if it were
some great accomplishment to have escaped
the rounds of death that men must die?

114

I know, my friends, that truth is in the words
I'll speak, but it has always been hard
and contested, this march of Faith into men's souls.

115

There is an old condition, a decree of Gods

eternal and sealed with extensive oaths,
that if a spirit blessed with long-lasting life
should by sin or error defile itself
with slaughter, or forswear an oath
in the spirit of Strife, he shall wander
      thirty thousand years
            apart from the blest,
born through time in various mortal forms,
switching through the painful tracks of life.
The air
      haunts them into the sea
         the sea
spits them onto the land
        the earth
spurns them into the sun
      and the sunlight
beats them into whirling air,
      passed on by all
hated by each,
      and I am one of them,
a fugitive from God, a wanderer
captivated by maniacal Strife

116

abhorring intolerable Necessity.

117

I have already been
    a bush and a bird
    a boy and a girl
      a mute fish in the sea

118

From what great happiness and honor
fallen to earth to move with humankind

119

We came to the cave

120

wept and moaned
at the strangeness of the place

121

a wasteland
where Murder and Spite and other species of doom,
withering diseases and rotting decay,
wander downshade through the meadows of sin.

122

There were Earth-Mother
and sunfaced Virgin,
there were blood-red Deris
and grave-eyed Harmony,
Lovely and Loathsome
Swift and Slow
Certainty loveable and dark-eyed Confusion

123

Growth and Wither, Rest and Awake
Motion and Firmness, and Stature with crowns
Defilement, and Silence, and Sound

124

and O god
what a miserable race humans are
to have sprung from such groans and contentions.

125

From the living he made the dead
changing their forms
and from the dead the living

126

clothing them in the unfamiliar
tunic of flesh

127

and when animals
they become lions
with lairs in the mountains
sleeping on the ground
and when trees
laurels

128

Ares was not their god, nor Kydoimos,
not Zeus their lord, nor Kronos, nor Poseidon
but only Kypris was their queen
> appeased with pious gifts
> painted icons, subtle perfumes
> sacrifice of merest myrrh, fumes
> of frankincense, libations spilled,
> yellow honey to earth
her altar unstained of bulls' bled gore,
this accounted the greatest defilement,
for men to reft the body's life
and eat the good limbs.

129

One man among them
> of extensive knowledge
and endless wealth of understanding
was master of every sort of learned art.
When he reached out with all his visceral mind
he easily perceived each and every existent
for ten and even twenty ages of man.

130

All creatures were tame   and gentle to men
all animals and birds   and loving minds glowed.

131

deathless Muse:

if for the sake of a single mortal being
you have admitted my work to your meditative care

                stand by me now
        O Kalliopeia I pray,
make my poem now a mirror to the gods in their bliss.

132

Prosperous: the man who has his fortune
                in godlike thoughts.
Destitute: who invests in dark speculation
        about the immortals.

133

        Impossible to bring It
        within our eyes' field
        or for hands to hold,
                that high, easy road
        by which belief

                        drops into men's minds

134

        It is not endowed
        with a human body or head,
        It has no arms
                branching out from a back
        no feet or fast knees

no shaded genitals:
                    It is one awesome Mind
                              inexpressibly alone
                    and riddling the universe
                    with its lightspeed thoughts.

                    135

Universal law

                    a continuum through the aether
                    through the infinite brightness

                    136

Won't you stop the cacophony of killing
                    Don't you see
you are mangling each other
          in your mindlessness?

                    137

The father lifts his son (changed
only in form) and slaughters him
with an idiot prayer
                         victims throng
          beseech the sacrificers
                    the attendants uneasy
but deaf to their cries he slaughters his son
there in his halls and prepares the ghastly
banquet.
               And the son seizes the father
               children their mother, tear
               out the life, eat dear flesh

138

draining life with bronze

139

and O
a pitiless day should have destroyed me
before contemplating such crime
                              this food to my lips

140

Abstain from Apollonian leaves, from laurel

141

from beans,
            lost souls

142

whom the roofed hall of aegis-bearing Zeus
will never receive, nor vengeful Hekate

143

cutting water from five fountains
with lasting bronze

144

fast from sin

145

since preplexed with hard evils
you will never ease your heart of its pain

yet in the end become prophets, singers of hymns,
healers and men prominent in public affairs
and last bud into gods mighty in honors

147

at the hearth and tables of the gods
free from human pains, immune, ageless.

148

Earth, our mortal context

149

pieced over with clouds

150

liver in blood

151

lifegiving

152

the senescence of the day

153

belly

Credit: Judy Roitman

Stanley Lombardo was born in New Orleans in 1943. He has received graduate degrees in classical studies from Tulane and the University of Texas. Currently he is a member of the faculty at the University of Kansas in Lawrence, where he lives with his wife and son.

Not wholly irrelevant to his work with the Greek philosophical poets is his Zen practice with the Korean master Seung Sahn, whose poetry he is now editing.

Printed in Great Britain
by Amazon